Chimpanzees

Kit Caudron-Robinson

Explore other books at:
WWW.ENGAGEBOOKS.COM

VANCOUVER, B.C.

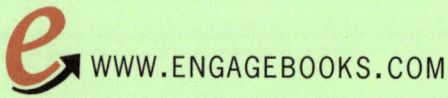

Chimpanzees: Level 3
Animals That Make a Difference!
Caudron-Robinson, Kit, 1996
Text © 2024 Engage Books
Design © 2024 Engage Books

Edited by: A.R. Roumanis,
Sarah Harvey, Melody Sun, and Ashley Lee
Design by: Mandy Christiansen

Text set in Arial Regular.
Chapter headings set in Nathaniel-19.

FIRST EDITION / FIRST PRINTING

All rights reserved. No part of this book
may be stored in a retrieval system, reproduced or transmitted in any form or by any other means without written permission from the publisher or a licence from the Canadian Copyright Licensing Agency. Critics and reviewers may quote brief passages in connection with a review or critical article in any media.

Page 19 bottom picture courtesy: National Science Foundation. Every reasonable effort has been made to contact the copyright holders of all material reproduced in this book.

LIBRARY AND ARCHIVES CANADA CATALOGUING IN PUBLICATION

Title: Chimpanzees / Kit Caudron-Robinson.
Names: Caudron-Robinson, Kit, author.
Description: Series statement: Animals that make a difference

Identifiers: Canadiana (print) 20230448542 | Canadiana (ebook) 20230448569
ISBN 978-1-77476-816-7 (hardcover)
ISBN 978-1-77476-817-4 (softcover)
ISBN 978-1-77476-818-1 (epub)
ISBN 978-1-77476-819-8 (pdf)
ISBN 978-1-77878-133-9 (audio)

Subjects:
LCSH: Chimpanzees—Juvenile literature.
LCSH: Human-animal relationships—Juvenile literature.

Classification: LCC QL737.P94 C38 2024 | DDC J599.885—DC23

This project has been made possible in part by the Government of Canada.

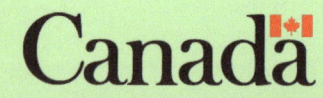

Contents

- 4 What Are Chimpanzees?
- 6 A Closer Look
- 8 Where Do Chimpanzees Live?
- 10 What Do Chimpanzees Eat?
- 12 How Do Chimpanzees Talk to Each Other?
- 14 Chimpanzee Life Cycle
- 16 Curious Facts About Chimpanzees
- 18 Kinds of Chimpanzees
- 20 How Chimpanzees Help Other Animals
- 22 How Chimpanzees Help Earth
- 24 How Chimpanzees Help Humans
- 26 Chimpanzees in Danger
- 28 How to Help Chimpanzees
- 30 Quiz

What Are Chimpanzees?

Chimpanzees are also called chimps. They are mammals. Mammals are animals with warm blood and bones in their backs.

Chimps are one of five kinds of Great Apes. Great Apes are **primates** with large brains and bodies. Chimps walk around on all four legs. They also get around by swinging from tree branches.

KEY WORD

Primates: a group of mammals with large brains and hands and feet that can grab things.

A Closer Look

Adult chimps weigh between 70 and 135 pounds (32 to 60 kilograms). They are 3 to 5.5 feet (1 to 1.7 meters) tall when standing up. The skin on their hands, face, and feet is black. The rest of their body is white.

Unlike monkeys, chimps do not have a tail.

Chimps have long, strong arms that hang down past their knees.

Chimps have large round faces. The only hair on their face is a small white beard.

Chimps have opposable thumbs that can move on their own. Opposable thumbs allow chimps to grab things and swing from branches.

Where Do Chimpanzees Live?

Chimps live in **tropical** forests and grasslands. They live in groups called communities. Some communities only have 10 chimps. Others can have over 100.

KEY WORD

Tropical: areas that are hot with lots of rain year round.

Chimps live in Western and Central Africa. They can be found between Senegal and Tanzania. There are more chimps in the Democratic Republic of Congo than anywhere else in Africa.

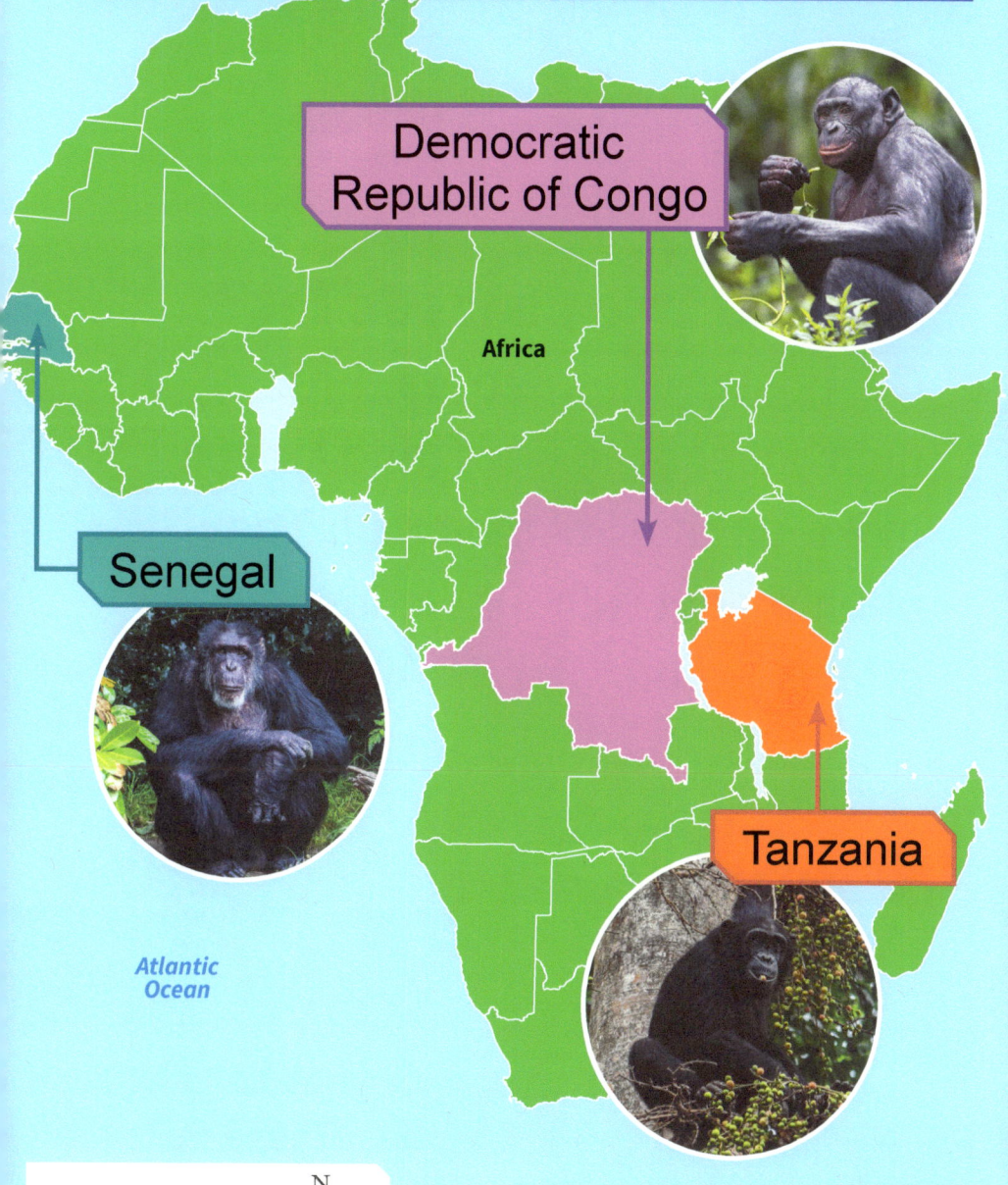

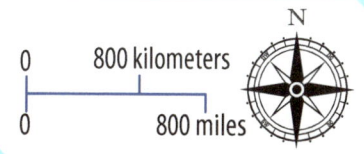

Democratic Republic of Congo

Senegal

Tanzania

Africa

Atlantic Ocean

0 — 800 kilometers
0 — 800 miles

N

Legend
Land
Ocean

What Do Chimpanzees Eat?

Chimps are **omnivores**. Fruit, nuts, insects, flowers, and leaves make up most of their diet. They often go out with others in their group and hunt for meat.

KEY WORD

Omnivores: animals that eat plants as well as other animals.

Chimps eat a lot of figs. These fruits are good for their health.

Chimps are one of the few animals in the wild that use tools. They smash open the hard shells of different nuts with rocks. Chimps also use long sticks to fish insects out of holes.

How Do Chimpanzees Talk to Each Other?

Chimps are very social. They form friendships by talking to each other. Chimps use their voice, face, and hands to talk.

When chimps pick insects off each other with their hands, they are also building friendships.

Like humans, chimps hold hands, kiss, and pat each other's backs to show kindness to each other. They call out with hoots, grunts, and screams to talk and tell others of danger. Communities work together to protect each other.

Chimpanzee Life Cycle

Adult female chimps have babies every five to six years. They have one or two babies at a time.

A baby chimp will hold on to the fur on its mother's belly for the first six months of its life. It will then ride on its mother's back for another year and a half.

14

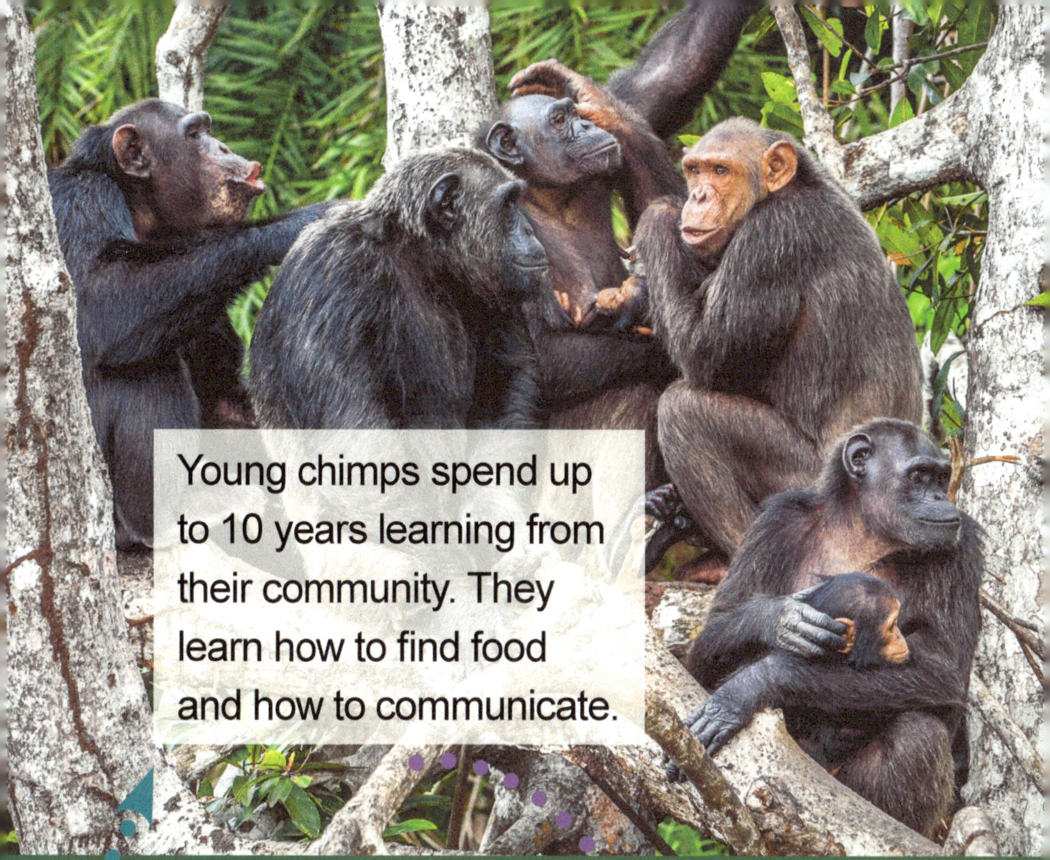

Young chimps spend up to 10 years learning from their community. They learn how to find food and how to communicate.

Male chimps usually stay with their home group their entire lives. Females often move to a nearby group to start a family. Most chimps live for about 45 years in the wild.

Curious Facts About Chimpanzees

One of the oldest chimps people know of was Little Mama. She lived into her 70s.

Chimps eat about 300 different types of food.

Chimps often make up games to play with each other when they are bored.

Some chimps have been taught sign language by humans.

Chimp fur is similar to the hair on human arms. It will only grow so long.

Chimps and other Great Apes can move their shoulders in more directions than most other animals.

Kinds of Chimpanzees

There are four kinds of chimps. Central chimpanzees live within the tropical rainforests of Central Africa. They are called "tschegos" by local people. "Tschegos" means laughter.

West African chimpanzees live in Western Africa. They use tools like wooden spears for hunting.

Eastern chimpanzees are the smallest kind of chimpanzee. They have rounder heads and darker skin than other chimps.

Nigeria-Cameroon chimpanzees live in forests across Nigeria and Cameroon. They have dark faces and long hair on the sides of their head and cheeks.

How Chimpanzees Help Other Animals

Scientists found that some chimps make friends with gorillas who live in the same areas. They help each other find food. Young chimps and gorillas also play with each other. This helps them learn how to communicate with others.

Chimps are a food source for animals like leopards and snakes. Leopards are one of the top **predators** of chimps. Without chimps, some animals would have less food.

KEY WORD

Predators: animals that hunt and eat other animals.

How Chimpanzees Help Earth

Chimps are an important part of the **ecosystem** where they live. The fruits they eat are filled with seeds. These seeds come out in their poop. Their poop helps the seeds grow and turn into new plants.

KEY WORD

Ecosystem: a community of living and nonliving things that work together to stay healthy.

Some chimps will travel long distances to find food. This helps seeds spread farther than they would be able to on their own. Plants are able to grow in new areas.

How Chimpanzees Help Humans

Chimps provide a lot of clues about how past humans lived. Dr. Jane Goodall is a scientist who has studied wild chimps for over 60 years. She found out that chimps make and use tools. This shows scientists how humans might have used tools millions of years ago.

Scientists also study how chimps talk to each other with gestures. They found out that humans can guess the meaning of those gestures. This helps scientists figure out how human language **evolved**.

KEY WORD

Evolved: changed over a long period of time to survive better in an environment.

Chimpanzees in Danger

A hundred years ago, there were a million chimps in Western Africa. Humans have been destroying forests as they build bigger farms and towns. This leads to **habitat loss**. The total population of wild chimps is now between 150,000 and 250,000.

KEY WORD

Habitat Loss: when the place plants and animals live is destroyed.

Chimps are in danger because they are hunted for their meat. Many wild chimps have been taken to zoos or circuses or used in medical research. Chimps are now listed as an **endangered** species.

KEY WORD

Endangered: an animal population that is at risk of dying off.

How to Help Chimpanzees

Many chimp forests are cut down so materials can be **mined** from the ground. These materials are used to make electronics like tablets and cell phones. Make sure to recycle your electronics so the materials can be used again. This will help protect the forests chimps live in.

KEY WORD

Mined: when useful materials are taken out of the ground.

Adopt a chimpanzee! You cannot take it home, of course. But many places that help save chimpanzees will send you a photo of your chimp and a certificate. The money from the adoption helps give food and homes to chimps in need.

Quiz

Test your knowledge of chimpanzees by answering the following questions. The questions are based on what you have read in this book. The answers are listed on the bottom of the next page.

1. How many species of Great Ape are there?

2. What was the name of one of the oldest chimps people know of?

3. What animal, other than humans, is the greatest threat to chimps?

4. Who is Dr. Jane Godall?

5. How many chimps are left in the world?

6. Are chimps endangered?

Explore other books in the Animals That Make a Difference series

Visit www.engagebooks.com to explore more Engaging Readers.

Answers: 1. Five 2. Little Mama 3. Leopards 4. A scientist who has studied wild chimps for over 60 years 5. Between 150,000 and 250,000 6. Yes

Milton Keynes UK
Ingram Content Group UK Ltd.
UKHW051902300524
443359UK00001B/3